AF316796

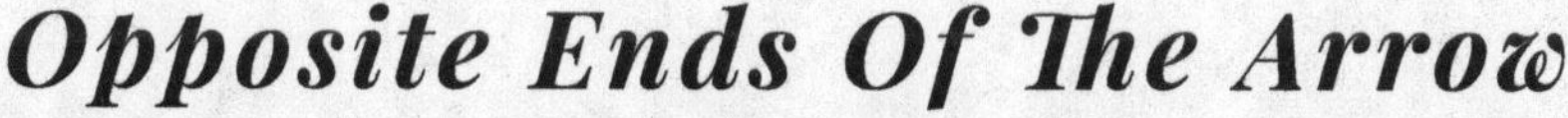

Opposite Ends Of The Arrow

Opposite Ends Of The Arrow

Jacob Z. Waldroup

IngramSpark

Contents

Contents

Contents

Dedication:

To all who have made this possible.
Thank you, truly from the depths of my being.
J.

Opposite Ends Of The Arrow

First we remembered, then went to war.
Now we deal with the aftermath of all it was for.

With any arrow comes opposite ends.
One where it ends, and one where it begins.

In our lives we deal with both love and loss.
This is the price we pay, this is life's cost.

A life without love is a life not lived.
A life without loss would be a gift.

Strength comes from pain.
What would life be without a little rain?

Coming down on us, washing us clean again.
Through our trials often come friends.

Those around who help us through.
Once unknown, now they're the glue.

That held us together so we wouldn't break.

JACOB Z. WALDROUP

Surviving the storm, feeling the earth shake.

Despite which end of the arrow you're living through,
don't be afraid to embrace this world anew.
As your path collides becoming part of the story of you.

Opposite ends of the arrow detailing our fate.
Leaving our hearts in an altered state.

{ 2 }

A Broken Heart Is Blind

Traveling westbound on the night train.
Nothing left here to gather, nothing left here to gain.

No longer knowing how we arrived here.
Nothing around us seemingly clear.

The heart is fickle, the heart is true.
The heart can be broken, shattered straight through.

If only there were a strong enough glue
to hold together the pieces throughout the night.
No reason to stay up, no reason to fight.

A broken heart is blind.
To what we know in our mind.

The flame between us had long burnt out.
Yet we sat here drowning alone in this drought.

Some days it feels that's when we can breathe.
Without you here, why am I suddenly relieved?

It's like a pressure has been lifted within.
Standing by waiting for something new to begin.

A Heart Gone Cold

Stacking wood preparing for the storm.
Keeping your home incandescently warm.

Until a gust of wind came putting out the fire.
Who's to blame for your lack of desire?

Putting out the flames with your frigid touch.
You always knew it meant so much.

Yet you left me alone.
Living in fear of the unknown.

What's to come, who could know?
As the fire had gone out, with a heart gone cold.

{ 4 }

Alone As I Wept

My fingers don't work like they use to before.
My vision faded as you closed the door.

My hands are numb, my heart is sore.
You stood there and watched as I fought this war.

With nothing left to say, nothing left to do.
I had to find it within myself to get over you.

You left me in a world forever blue.
No longer knowing what to do.

How could I continue without you here?
For the past four years you'd always been near.

Near to my heart, body, and soul.
Please someone tell me, where did the love go?

What was once a castle built from stone.
Has since been left empty, and now overgrown.

I could't believe when I heard the news.

You'd been seeing others at night while I slept.
Now you've left me here alone as I wept.

An Invitation Which Never Came

Unwilling to accept that final goodbye.
Time would continue to pass you by.

Eight years you'd sit there, life on hold.
Waiting for something, what you didn't know.

I guess in life some feelings are that strong.
You knew you loved them, it had been them all along.

Could they not see, you were always alone.
Waiting for them to come back home.

No moment was wasted waiting by the phone.
Hoping that one day they'd surely call.

Inviting you to have coffee, easing the pain.
Yet that would remain an invitation which never came.

As the days passed by, the nights grew colder.
You'd wake one day to find yourself older.

Eight years you'd waited, when they were long gone.
What were you doing? This had to be wrong.

Finally taking that candle from the window which you lit every
night.
Hoping they'd rush to you from the sight of its light.

Letting them know you'd never gone.
You had been there waiting, all along.

Finally accepting that day wouldn't arrive.
You blew out the candle, which kept that hope alive.

{ 6 }

Burn Another Page

Another night, another fight.
Taking up another page in the diary of your life.

These entries are written in red to signify the rage.
With the intent of healing, it comes time to burn another page.

Feelings put into words, and swept across a page.
Allowing you the author, to relinquish all emotion
setting your soul free, from the burden it's bore for so long.

Taking the memories of the moments that have passed.
Expelling them from your mind, to place in this world.

Only temporary, as you've completed another entry.
You tear out the page, opening the drawer next to you.

Finding the matches you seek, throwing the page into the bin.
Striking the match, lighting it up again.

Sitting there watching, you deeply exhale.
Those memories no longer haunting,
as you've sent them straight to hell.

So light it up, and burn another page.
This is your life, this is your stage.

{ 7 }

Burning The Past

Strike the match burn it down.
Watch the ashes fall to the ground.

That was the moment you truly knew.
They were the one who had done for you
what no one else could do.

Setting a blaze to the past which had imprisoned you for ages.
Now you're free to create new pages.

Of the story which you'll live.
Finding a love, learning to forgive.

All the things letting them go.
Burning the past allowed you to do so.

{ 8 }

Can't Find A Pulse

Standing out in the pouring rain.
Under an awning awaiting the night train.

I saw someone who looked like you.
Only their eyes were green, where yours are blue.

Suddenly I remembered like a flash in the night.
I had lost all control, no sense of sight.

Taken back as if I were there.
Feeling the breeze blowing through my hair.

Looking on I watched it again.
Like an old movie at home with a friend.

Only this wasn't of the humorous kind.
More like a horror playing out in my mind.

Standing there watching you leading me on.

I can't find a pulse I was no longer breathing.
Standing there in silence I realize I'm bleeding.

My heart was broken, pouring blood like a spout.
Draining my veins slowly dying no doubt.

The memory of us fades as the world turns black.
Suddenly like lightning here I am back.

Startled I realize my train had arrived.
It was the memory of us in which I had died.

{ 9 }

Cigarette Smoke & Infidelity

From the garden I ran.
Seeking to hold your hand.

Dropping all I held.
Knowing deeply we'd failed.

Thinking I saw you standing at the window above.
I froze at the door giving myself a shove.

I enter the room my breath I kept.
Knowing your feet had already been swept.

By the one you now call home.
Yet there I stood forever alone.

The smell in the room lingered.
It was clear you'd just slipped through my fingers.

As cigarette smoke and infidelity clang to my skin.
Knowing your heart would never be mine again.

I left as I came.

JACOB Z. WALDROUP

Walking out into the rain.

I fall to my knees.
Begging please.

For the sky to wash away
the smell of cigarette smoke and infidelity.

Which now my senses consumed.
I knew I could never renter that room.

Closure

Looking out a window watching life pass by.
It had been so many months now I no longer cry.

I sat in this chair rocking back and forth for so long.
Why am doing this to myself over someone who done me wrong?

I knew it was crazy after what had been done.
A betrayal so deep, worse than the burn of the sun.

I knew I couldn't continue as such.
A sense of closure was needed so much.

Until the day it came to me so.
I realized the closure was in the act of betrayal.

A sense of closure wasn't to come.
Nor did I need it after what you had done.

I then decided the time wasted was enough.
I rose from that chair quickly gathering my stuff.

Emerging from that room after seemingly so long.

It was time to move on with my life getting over you.

The only regret I now feel.
Is the time I wasted looking out that window with my life sitting
still.

Deception By Omission

Waiting for a coffee down the street.
A place held dear, where one day you'll meet.

Someone you'd give your heart to.
Never expecting the things you'd go through.

As things began to surface.
Their truth you'd find.

A deception by omission which would change your fate.
Leaving your well-being in an altered state.

Thinking you knew them it came as a shock.
Upon finding out their reality you felt hit by a rock.

How could anyone create such an intricate web of lies?
Given our history, does this come as a surprise?

It's wild to think how someones truth.
Can turn you into an ammeter sleuth.

If it hadn't been for you, how much deeper would this have gone?

Aren't you glad, you threw that first stone?

Into the pond, searching out their details.
A story throughout time, which never ceases to fail.

Dishonesty Of Silence

The quitting bell sounds as the sun rises.

Another shift over stocking shelves at the store.
Another days pay on the books, feeding your family once more.

Going home to those who wait for you there.

Waiting for you to walk in with that smile.
The one only you could present with such style.

Yet as the door opened there wasn't a sound.
The house was quite no one around.

Where have they gone? You wonder setting your stuff down.
Stepping out on the porch looking down at the ground.

Unable to see if their car was there.
You stood frozen all you could do was stare.

What's going on? You wonder looking around,
Not a single possession of theirs to be found.

You see your story may lack original detail.
For this relationship you'd long known you had failed.

It was only this day they gathered the strength.
To take their belongings no need to return.

As the dishonesty of your silence had given you away.
They knew they could no longer justify a reason to stay.

The betrayal was deeper than you could have ever known.
You never thought this far to the day they were gone.

On the table there was a note.

It read:

You'll never know the sting of this burn
I loved you so deeply I couldn't believe
The reason I'm leaving I only found out last eve.
How could you do this? I'll never know.
When did your heart become colder than snow?
Did you ever love me? Was it all a show?
What was your goal here? Do I want to know?
Wasn't there something we could have done?
Bringing us closer, together as one?
Why didn't you talk to me?
We could have talked this through.
Now I'm no longer breathing.
My blood runs blue.
I couldn't find a reason to stay.
As soon as I heard the world turned gray.
Why did this happen? Wasn't I enough?
Why didn't I see it? The signs were there.

Opposite Ends Of The Arrow

The way you touched me, the part in your hair.
The changes were subtle, the flags were red.
I had no reason to think ahead.
I didn't think we'd ever be here.
I had no time to prepare, not a moment to fear.
Yet I can no longer remain with you here.
What you have done burns my soul.
Blackening my heart, turning it cold.
Just as cold as I imagine yours to be.
Why did you do this?
To me...

That's where the note ended.

As they dropped it to the floor.
Falling to their knees they weren't so sure.

That it had been worth it for a moment of pleasure.
They've lost their world no bond to tether.

Yet were they sorry? They'd never know.
They as so many couldn't see past the show.

That they put on for so long like a suit.
They gave up the game foregoing pursuit.

Tucking their tail they'd never reach out.
Looking back on these days barely surviving the drought.

They never imagined the dishonesty of their silence
would lead them here.
Losing it all, everything they held dear.

Easy Loving You

From the moment that we met.
I felt a feeling I hadn't yet.

There was something, the look in your eye.
The feeling in my heart, a flame which wouldn't die.

A love which burned from that moment on.
As the world turned, fear which had gone.

It was always easy loving you.

Picking up the phone calling again.
You truly were my very best friend.

I knew in life with you by my side.
There was no reason to wonder, no reason to hide.

My feelings for you only ever grew.
It was always easy loving you.

Everything I Am

Met on a Sunday down by the creek.
You were sitting there laughing at something you'd read.

I knew from that moment I had to know you.
The one with such an infectious laugh.

It was from that moment on, which I'll never look back.
As I traverse this life with you by my side.

I give you everything that I am, and everything I'm not.
To bring joy to your life, is all that I've sought.

Since that day, down by the creek.
The day which fate allowed us to meet.

Forever Is Tonight

Meeting you must have been fate.
Allowing our paths to align here on this date.

What are the odds both you and I.
Would be at the very same place, at the very same time?

Standing in front of this fountain.
Watching the moon dance across the sky.

A clock tower chiming in the distance.
Welcoming in the midnight hour.

When the clouds began to release,
down upon us from the sky.

Looking over at you I say
"looks like we're in for a shower."

Grabbing my hand you usher me towards
the awning of a quaint cafe.

Looking into your eyes as your body pressed against mine.

Opposite Ends Of The Arrow

I couldn't help but feel the passion wash over.

Sending sparks into the street.
Had a complete, and total stranger just swept me off my feet?

This was the moment in which I ask your name.
With it you whisper gently forever is tonight
igniting our eternal flame.

Four Forty Two

It was at four forty two I knew I was through.
Dealing with this shit, dealing with you.

Why couldn't you see? Left forever blue.
It was on a Friday at four forty two.

Looking back in time.
I could say the same.

It was at four forty two that I knew I loved you.

Sitting there texting, too shy to speak on the phone.
Falling a bit deeper with each sound of the tone.

Four forty two a time I'll hold dear.
Knowing you'd always be near.

If not with me in my heart you'll remain.
It was at four forty two that blood rushed through every vein.

With my heart coming alive again.
A life with you I was ready to begin.

{ 17 }

Frozen (Suspended In Love With You)

For years your life stood frozen.
Going through the motions of the day.

Standing still as the world passed you by.
Unbeknownst to you how the time would fly.

One day you realize as you look in the mirror.
The person before you was no longer young.

You'd spent your life searching for a song which was sung.
Thinking back on the many years prior.

You realize you had stood there frozen suspended in love with you.
That person you'd long ago given your heart to.

Hoping that flame had continued to burn.
You hadn't realized, you'd missed your turn.

They were long gone.
As was your youth.

You'd spent your years waiting.
Unable to accept the truth.

Now looking back, it hit you like a boulder.
Beginning to fall, you feel a grasp on your shoulder.

Looking back to find no one was there.
It was you in your mind your burden to bare.

Accepting the reality of what once was.
You know it's time to become something more.

Finally closing that long chapters door.

Hollow Promises

Whispering gently into your ear.
Things you'd been so longing to hear.

Telling you their plans, down to the smallest detail.
Unbeknownst to you, these were lies without fail.

Empty words would leave their mouth.
As hollow promises would come, and go.

Everything they were telling you.
Yeah, that was all for show.

Taking a risk, they said what you wanted to hear.
Hoping you'd believe them, drawing you in near.

Letting down your defenses.
You'd no longer fear.

Being with them, as your hopes would distract.
Taking advantage this was their moment to act.

Taking what they wanted.

JACOB Z. WALDROUP

Their words fallen on deaf ears.

Hollow promises, you'd believe.
Those things which you'd dreamed, you'd never receive.

Hollow promises can break our hearts.
Making us pause, before giving another a start.

—

{ 19 }

If You Want To

If you want to, I'll remain by your side.
If you want to, I'll no longer hide.

If you want to, I'll see this day through with you.
If you want to, I'll paint your world any other color than blue.

If you want to, we can pack a bag and go away.
If you want to, we can light a fire and stay.

If you want to, I'll buy you that ring.
If you want to, we'll ask your mama to sing.

If you want to, we'll build this life together.
If you want to, I'll stay with you through forever.

{ 20 }

Like A Book

Tomorrow's a mystery, but we've got history.
Didn't even need to look, to read you like a book.

That smirk wreaking of guilt,
with the arrogance of thinking you'd gotten with it.

Remember your lack of empathy, when my sun fell out of the sky?
I remember your lack of sympathy when all I could do was cry.

You standing there looking down at me on my knees again.
Begging you to love me, yet you continue to pretend.

Would you rather I just go?
My names not Keith, I'm not just another Joe.

Fuck that guy, really what a piece of shit.
How could I beg you to love me, when you can't even tolerate it?

My love, I've given in abundance.
Yet you've managed to move just out of the way.

Treating me as if I were some sort of dance.

Opposite Ends Of The Arrow

Tell me why did I risk it all to give you another chance?

When all you've done has been watching as I fall time, and time
again.
At this point, I don't think we could even be friends.

So why am I here? Why do I stay?
Why can't I pack a bag running away?

My mind knows the reality, yet my hearts still trapped in chains.
Will I ever break free? Or will I die a victim of your games?

Just one look, I read you like a book. I knew then, this would never
end.

Linger Like A Daydream

Dreaming of you came without thought.
For my heart was a fight which you once fought.

Sitting beside me no one was there.
It was as if you had vanished into thin air.

I search for you not knowing where you'd gone.
Knowing in my heart something was wrong.

Running in slow motion, clocks ticking in reverse.
I sit there hopelessly feeling as if I'd been cursed.

Opening my mouth words would come no more.
No matter how hard I pushed I couldn't open the door.

I could hear you laughing as I see your shadow on the floor.
I knew it was you I'd always adore.

When I notice your shadow become two.
I couldn't believe it, there was someone in there with you.

Who could it be, what were they there for?

Opposite Ends Of The Arrow

Fucking dammit, why can't I open this door?

I began knocking pounding my flesh on the wood.
Still seeing your shadows neither of you stood.

Why wouldn't you come, could you hear me knocking?
Perhaps there's a key I could use for unlocking.

I turn to search no longer in front of the door I stood.
Yet here in a hallway, this couldn't be good.

Where am I now? Where did that door go?
Who was that with you? A friend or a foe?

How can I find you when I'm there no more.
I have to find my way back in front of that door.

I began to run down this long hall.
Seemingly never ending that's when I began to fall.

Nothing beneath me, the floor no longer there.
I was trapped suspended frozen in midair.

I could feel my breathing becoming slight.
How can I make it through this dark night?

That's when I heard it, a voice calling my name,
I woke to realize it had all been a game.

My mind had been playing on me once more.
You were long gone, yet your memory lingers like a daydream.

Haunting me deeply as time continues to pass.

Sometimes it feels like I'm encased within glass.

Standing there pounding against its walls.
Yet no one can hear me, not even one of my calls.

In a sea of people who continue to walk by.
The air became thick as I started to fly.

The memory of you, and the daydreams that came.
I finally released you taking with you this pain.

Little One

Little one, you're the one I won't get to know.
Little one, pictures of you I don't get to show.

Little one, there isn't a day I'm not thinking of you.
Little one, you were truly one of the few.

Little one, you painted my sky the brightest blue.
Little one, since that day it lost its hue.

Little one, your name was already written there.
Little one, to not know you isn't fair.

Little one, your heart beat remains in rhythm with mine.
Little one, I had to let you go, be free now with the divine.

Little one, there will come a day we'll get to meet.
Little one, how I yearn to hear the patter of your feet
as they cross the wooden floor.

Little one, your memory is all I live for.
Little one, your soul I'll always adore.

Little one, until that day please know.
Little one, I'm with you now, and forever so.

{ **23** }

Lost At Sea

I was lost at sea, until you saved me with just one look.
For me to know I loved you, that is all it took.

The waves crashing against the boat, in the midst of this storm.
Who was that standing there? Why am I suddenly so warm?

Could you have known, when we set out from shore.
This would be the moment we each were searching for.

Deep within each our own soul.
Lighting our fires hotter than any coal.

Either of us had felt before.
Knowing we'd found the cure.

For those lonely nights.
Brought on by sadness, and fright.

Each lost at sea, until our ship came in.
The right place, at the right time is all it took.
Meeting you there that day, my entire world shook.

Nightmares Tell Tales

Nightmares tell tales our conscious refuses to hear.
Whispers of truths confirming our fears.

Waking up gasping, begging for air.
Am I safe now? Was I really there?

Checking the time on the clock, beaming light into the dark.
Unwittingly processing creating a spark.

What was once a fear, has now been lived.
Could I handle it? Do I have that to give?

Was it a warning? I begin to think.
Was my body telling me something?
Is my armor as the shell of a tank?

What if my fear manifests into real life?
Do I have the strength to pull out the knife?

That had been plunged into my back.
By a dear loved one who's confidence I lack.

Knowing I could never do that to them.
What draws the line deep within?

Here I'm left pacing, wiping the sweat from my brow.
Was my ship sinking, going down by the bow?

Passing the window, peering out.
Seeing the leaves wilt before me as if in a drought.

Shaking it off I lie back down.
Remembering for now I'm safe and sound.

Nightmares tell tales we dare not to dream.
Yet is it all as bad as it might seem?

Goodnight.

{ 25 }

No Need To Look

The sound of the tone coming from your phone.
In the other room I already knew.

No need to look to know there was
from ear to ear bursting within.
A grin so wide immersed in sin.

No need to look to know plans were made.
Soon your presence here would surely fade.

No need to look to know their name.
It didn't matter it was all a game.

For you that is getting away with it, or so you thought.
You never knew you were already caught.

That's right my dear, I've known for a while now.
The need to fear lies behind my smile now.

You see I've known since that day.
You slipped up in the way,
you looked at me as you entered the door.

It was a look I'd seen many times before.

The look of guilt written across your face.
They were the one who took my place.
In the bed with you face to face.

I could smell the cologne from across the room.
No need to confirm, no need to resume.

The conversation from all the times before.
I knew the moment you walked through that door.

{ 26 }

Numb

I'm told it's shock this feeling of nothing.
Still in my heart I cry out to feel something.

What once was there is no longer told.
I stand here frozen as my blood runs cold.

This feeling of numb, no longer alive.
As if something within me had surely died.

The loss of you suddenly so.
Has left me empty with nowhere to go.

What once was a path we were on together.
One which I thought led to forever.

Now I know I'm on this road alone.
Learning to live without you now that you're gone.

Replaced By Them

Temptation, never far.
Ready to leave its mark, creating a scar.

No matter where we may go.
It's always watching, waiting to show.

Flashing lights bringing you in.
Ready to seduce you, poisoning from within.

What it may be, proverbial sin.
Feeling great from the moment that it begins.

Yet its power will fade I promise.
One day you'll realize you've been dishonest.

You've stepped out on your partner.
Unbeknownst to them.

You're now conflicted filled with fear.
Which one of them would you rather have here?

How did this happen, was this really your life?

You knew in your heart that for this to happen.

You'd have to break the news.
They were being replaced by them, the one you'd surely choose.

Leaving your partner of years
Not giving them a warning, nor reason to fear.

You strike like lightning breaking the news.
You cannot blame them for being confused.

What you had done wasn't the first of its kind.
Temptation had bit you controlling your mind.

Giving you the choice which you had to choose.
What to give up, and what to lose.

You chose this feeling, a world brand new.
Yet a life you destroyed, unprepared to live through.

One day happy the next replaced by them.
Was it worth it, the pleasure of sin?

Saturday Nights For Loving You

Saturday night, always felt right.
Coming or going, it didn't matter.

The more time spent with you.
The more they were flattered.

You took them to a place higher than high.
As you reached past the stars, beyond the sky.

From that night on Saturday nights became for loving you.
Many adventures in a world of color.

Faster, and faster until falling to the ground.
Lying there in the grass as if no one were around.

Taking your hand they pulled you in.
Now that was a kiss you'd always defend.

Your heart grew several sizes that day.
Swoon by those feelings, deep within.

That's when you knew, they were more than a friend.

{ 29 }

Seasons Of The Heart

As the seasons change.
We tend to change with them.

No different is the seasons of the heart.
Winter, Spring, Summer, Autumn/Fall, and into winter again.

The changes of the phases of our lives.
Reflected like a mirror within our soul.

The only way out is through.
With each change of season, comes a differing hue.

To your life, and all that surround.
Some bring ups, as some bring downs.

None of us can ever know.
Whether the day will bring sun, or snow.

Life, fickle, and often unkind.
The changing of the season, much like the changing of the mind.

Within the seasons of the heart there is no dictation of time.

Some having to bare the brunt of them in the hours between
sleeps.

We never know, which one might show.
As we continue to go.

About our days, within this maze called life.
The seasons of the heart can bring joy, as well as strife.

30

Simply A Bad Feeling

Was I still dreaming, was this real?
Were you out seeking some sort of thrill?

Remaining unknown, you probably thought you'd be alone.

You never expected to find me here.
Did they do it for you, did they my dear?
Did they help you finally conquer that fear?

The fear of never feeling again.
The fear of losing me, the fear of that sin.

The fear of falling from a tall something.
The fear of becoming simply nothing.

The fear of turning the knob to find.
The only reason you'd change your mind.

I knew you'd have to see the look on my face.
To feel the shame, to realize the disgrace.

I knew it would take my intervention.

All this due to lovers intuition.

You see what finally brought me here.
Was simply a bad feeling, that was all my dear.

The connection between us, a lovers bond.
Sensing the feeling from beyond.

You may not know it, but I can look at your face.
Reading your emotions like looking into a case.

Full of pages, protected by glass.
I could read for ages, even teach a class.

That's how connected to me we still are.
I can sense your inhibition even from a far...

It wasn't easy, nor was it hard.
To come to the conclusion, the sleight of the card.

As I uncovered slowly the truth.
Using skills which I mastered like some sort of sleuth...

Now we're here alone in this room.
A room which would be all too soon.

Filled with hatred, blood on the walls.
From the lashing of tongues with disgust as it falls.

All these secrets pouring out.
How did I not realize we were in such a drought?

To me I hadn't even considered anything was wrong.

Opposite Ends Of The Arrow

That your feelings had withered like spring flowers
on autumns window seal.
Giving up my fight, losing my will.

I had been consumed with my own distress.
This my dear I must confess.

I know you aren't the only one to blame.
I know to you this wasn't some game.

I had left you feeling ever so lonely.
Going through the motions like some sort of zombie.

I hadn't considered you'd taken to heart.
The way I was feeling as if you played a part.

You see it was never even about you.
It was always me, I was that hue.

Of gray which we painted that wall.
It was both our faults causing our tower to fall.

All of this based simply on a bad feeling.
Tell me is this our fate that we're sealing?

31

So I Left

I never cared for the month of July.
Though I never imagined it'd leave me without a dry eye.

All in the span of a week or two.
My world was turned over, I'd find myself without you.

First our home was taken in vain.
No matter the struggle, nor the pain.

Forced to move hours away.
Longing to be with you each moment of the day.

Then it happened the nightmares came.
A feeling deep, I'd never be the same.

Unable to shake the wonder in my mind.
I took to the web to seek what I could find.

There it was in streaming color.
The nightmares vision coming true.

On the screen in front of me was a picture of you.

Opposite Ends Of The Arrow

With the caption of what you sought.

Realizing then I was right to be distraught.
All my fears had entered the world.

Things I couldn't say aloud.
Now staring me in the face, feeling alone in a crowd.

So many questions entered my mind.
Was there more, or was this enough for me to find?

It didn't matter, I knew it was over.
So I left without looking over my shoulder.

You wanted to know why.
So I told you.

You began to cry.
Instantly I began to wonder why.

Were you crying because of your betrayal?
Or were you crying because you were caught?

Either way, we were over.
The damage was done, the war was fought.

Only in this battle the win was the loss.
Neither side claiming victory, as each had failed.
Now I sit alone here, longing to be held.

{ 32 }

Stage One Of Grief (Denial)

When they told me you had gone.
I told them no, they must be wrong.

There was no way you left me here.
Alone without you, drowning in fear.

I left the room shaking my head.
There was no way you were what they said.

I took out my phone dialing your number over and over to no
avail.
Leaving message after message filling your voicemail.

Come on answer I repeat over and over.
There's no way, you said you were sober.

As the hours pass still in disbelief.
I'm sure I'll reach you not knowing that was the grief.

I didn't know then I was in denial.
What came next was like being on trial.

Opposite Ends Of The Arrow

Nothing felt real, nothing at all.
For days I stayed by the phone waiting for the moment you'd call.

A call which never came.
A life gone, with mine rearranged.

{ 33 }

Stage Two Of Grief (Anger)

When that call never came I didn't know who I could blame.
All I knew is that I was filled with anger.

A rage burned deeper than I'd ever known.
Admitting you'd been taken saying aloud that you'd gone.

I couldn't bring myself to blame you for leaving.
I looked everywhere in panic I began dry heaving.

Eventually falling to the floor.
Feeling like I could breathe no more.

I couldn't form a single word.
Only tears and whispers came out into the world.

I knew eventually I'd be okay.
I also knew that wouldn't be today.

{ 34 }

Stage Three Of Grief
(Bargaining)

Standing just outside the room.
My heart sank, filled with gloom.

Hearing the sound of the alarm bells ring.
On the countless number of machines.

That were once keeping you here.
It can't be over now, can it my dear?

How can you really be gone?
We were just talking, as if nothing were wrong.

Walking away, forcing myself to believe.
You weren't gone, you were still here with me.

Numerous people try, and stop me as I walk.
I brush past them unable to talk.

It wasn't the time, nor the place.
I wasn't able to accept this, seeing the looks on their face.

It made it too real, something that I wasn't near ready to feel.
Why couldn't they see, I wasn't there yet?

I couldn't believe it to be true.
I ran down the hall trying to find you.

I stumble into a room, you weren't there.
Falling down begging God, why, this can't be fair...

What ever it takes, take me instead.
I'll be the offering, here my head.

Take the blood from my veins, take the breath from my lungs.
Please dear God, take me. I'm the one.

Not you...
Never you...

How can I go on living without you here?
Haven't we been through enough this year...

Slowly rising as the tears began to fall.
I hear the footsteps of someone coming through the door from the
hall.

This time allowing them to hold me.
Catching me so I wouldn't fall.

It came pouring out, very unexpected.
My best try at bargaining had done no good.

I have to stay here...

When it should be you.

I'll never be the same.
As all color left the room.

35

Stage Four Of Grief (Depression)

Sitting in this room, which used to be ours.
There's no longer laughter, or the lighting of fires.

In the dark with only light from the crack in the door.
Why am I still here, what's worth continuing for?

Now that you're gone, I can't imagine coming home.
To this place we built as ours.

Twenty Seven years we spent in this place.
There isn't a nook nor cranny which I can't see your face.

Every inch of every room the memory of us entirely consumes.
I want so for that to bring comfort, but it's only brought pain.

Pain I'm not ready to feel again.
For now I keep all the lights off.

Perhaps if I can't see it, it isn't true.
One day I'll hear it, the door open its you.

I know that's foolish. I know that you're gone.
Yet my hearts not ready, to feel at home.

Since the moment you left, the depression set in.
Unable to find comfort in any family or friend.

The days grew long, and the nights grew colder.
I have no desire to be another day older.

Not without you, here by my side.
My only goal now is to lay here and hide.

36

Stage Five Of Grief
(Acceptance)

Though it had been many years since you'd gone.
I finally found peace in all that was wrong.

It wasn't easy, nor did I think the day would come.
It had been so long, since I'd truly seen the sun.

It's funny how it happens.
One day you're in this pain you can't see a way to end.
Then it just happens, you slowly begin again.

Even if you don't realize at first.
Taking small steps here on earth.

Picking yourself up one inch at a time.
Now you're running miles in a warmth sublime.

Though you didn't realize you'd done the thing you swore you
couldn't.
You accepted their fate, and that it couldn't be yours.

Opposite Ends Of The Arrow

You had to let go in order to absorb.
All the light which entered the room.
Allowing you to blossom into full bloom.

Acceptance, the final stage.
Often the hardest turn of the page.

{ 37 }

Standing Near The Towers Edge

Watching the cards fall down like rain.
As the table was flipped in anger again.

Slowly standing with the chaos around.
Calmly walking away on the terrace you'd be found.

Standing there near the towers edge.
Inching closer to the ledge.

Looking down at the peace of the grounds.
The leaves blowing gently in the breeze.

The madness behind you all the while.
They'd found out about him, Kyle.

An affair which had gone on so long.
Leaving no trace, seemingly unknown.

Yet during the game you let it slip.
A minor detail, the smallest of them.

Their growing suspicions were simply confirmed.
Flipping the table now it's their turn.

Although you thought there were no signs.
There were gaps in the scheme of time.

Little moments, you didn't realize they saw.
The sparkle in your eye looking into the distance.
They knew there was something you were reminiscent.

Although they thought it, they didn't allow their mind to go there.
That couldn't happen to them, not you who'd had an affair.

Surely it was all just in their mind.
There was no tangible evidence they could find.

Until today, when you unknowingly unraveled a lie.
They knew then for sure, there was another guy.

As you stand there near the towers edge.
You contemplate jumping down into the hedge.
Knowing that wasn't ever the answer,
you turn back towards the tower looking in.
There you saw it, the look on their face the result of your sin.

Sting Of The Pain (Doesn't Wash Away)

It isn't the alarm clock by the bed
that wakes you these days, is it baby?

Up pacing the halls, coffee in hand,
the ticking of an old clock in the room somewhere nearby.
Yet you don't hear a thing above your own thoughts, do you baby?

Turning the faucet running your hand through its decent to the
base of the tub.
Checking the temperature before entering the shower again,
yet it isn't getting clean that's on your mind, is it baby?

Try as hard as you may the sting of the pain doesn't wash away.
I'm sorry baby.

Though you made it through the war,
the memories of what was lost on both sides of the battle
stay with you as you go about your days, don't they baby?

With each sudden remembrance of the smallest detail

bringing you directly back to the midst of the pain.
Feeling each infliction of the pain upon you by the one you once
called home.
It's unbearable isn't it baby?

It's often said that getting through it is enough. That isn't true
though is it baby?

So few discuss aloud the baggage taken with once the dust settles,
and we begin to pick up the pieces of what was once home,
and that no matter how hard we try the sting of the pain simply
doesn't wash away...

Tell Me Why

Tell me why, I have to beg for your attention.
Tell me why, I seldom hear a mention.
Tell me why, being with you sometimes feels
like we're in a parallel dimension.

Tell me why, the light is gone in your eyes.
Tell me why, you're a master of disguise.

Tell me why, your blood runs cold.
Tell me why, you're no longer by my side as we grow old.

Tell me why, like a thief in the night my heart you came in and
stole.
Tell me why, to the highest bidder you then sold.
Tell me why, your heart went cold.

Tell me why, you let me go.
Tell me why, was it all for show?
Tell me why, was I supposed to know?

Tell me why, you no longer cry.
All I need now is for you to tell me why.

40

The Diary Of A Broken Heart

Dear Diary,

It's me again, old friend.
Another day has come, and gone.

This one wasn't as bad as some that have come.
Tomorrow will probably be different.
Especially when you're this lonesome.

Since the day they left. My heart has missed a beat.
Barely pumping enough blood, to keep me on my feet.

Time moves at a glacial pace.
Some days when the depressions bad, I can't even wash my face.

Going through the motions of what they say we do.
Lacking all emotion, living a life that's blue.

Since that day, the skies been gray.
Even to whisper their name, I haven't been able to say.

I guess as I write my thoughts in you,

You've become the diary of a broken heart.

Maybe one day, with the rise of the sun.
We'll set our life apart from these feelings.

So many that there are.
Finally moving on, doing better than we have so far.

41

The Fall

Middle of June, it came so soon.
Like the sun fading at the rise of the moon.

There isn't a day which it's forgotten.
The fall of the commemoratively down trodden.

Once those in positions of promise.
Now taken down by the undeniably dishonest.

In order to keep us lower than they.
Tending the gardens, bailing the hay.

All the things they wish not to do.
They're the ring masters, we're trapped in their zoo.

Little is there that we can do.
Isn't there someone? Tell me who.

Yet together we stand, taller than all the buildings in the land.
Come now my neighbor, take me by the hand.
Rising up against the man.
Taking back our place to stand.

Just like the plot in that series of books.
A war would ensue making us take a hard look.

Look at all that had come.
From the fall of the down trodden.
Someones daughter, and son.

If only greed, and sloth weren't allowed a place in power.
Perhaps we would be at peace this very hour...

Something to think about as we continue to remember.
The fall of our fathers, who once our world centered.

{ 42 }

The Games You Were Playing

Dressing up, dressing down.
Heading out on the town.

Left me here alone in fear, never asking me to go.
Yet, I know where, why, and so.

Why would you? These are the game you were playing.
The objective? Wholeheartedly betraying.

Our union, and what that stood for.
Another knife to the back, each time you step out the door.

Heading out to play your games.
Another faceless Jane, or John or whoever it might be that day.

These were the games you set out to play.
Taking with you a piece of my heart.

Leaving me here, unable to restart.
Shattered, empty, alone on the floor.

It wasn't about me.

I couldn't have done more.

No, this was all about you.
What you were going through.

I was just a pawn without a stake.
You were the one, who's love you's were fake.

How could you love someone, and do what you done?
That isn't possible, no way under the sun.

So many day's I've wandered aimlessly in a haze.
Unable to leave, because what is there left?

My entire existence, had been taken in the theft.
What do I do now? I didn't know.

So for now, it had to be so.
Until the day, I gathered the strength.

Suddenly better enough to pull rank.
Overthrowing you and your game.

That last time you went out?
I left without doubt.

You never knew, what happened to me.
I was on my own now, finally free.

Your game was over, you had lost.
Had I won, or paid the cost?

{ 43 }

The One Who

It's been over a month since I slept through the night.
As I sit and wait for you by the moons light.

Midnight, two, five, and seven are the times when.
My heart comes alive once again.

For that brief moment hearing your voice through the phone.
Im gently reassured nothing is wrong.

Soon I'll sleep in the light of day.
Yet through the night I continuously stay.

I stay by the phone awaiting your call.
I stay so you'll know I'm giving it my all.

I stay so the fire will continue to burn.
I stay so that one day it might be my turn.

I stay just in case you need a guide through a storm.
I stay so you'll know you have a place so warm.

I stay no matter how tired I might be.

I stay so that maybe you'll finally see.

It was me all along.
The one who was here waiting, the one who was strong.

The one who never left your side.
The one who refused to run and hide.

The one who was there through it all.
No matter how hard the stumble, no matter how far the fall.

The one who was hurt by your running around.
The one who was found lying on the ground.

The one who never gave up the fight.
The one who couldn't turn off the light.
The one who refused to sleep without you through the night.

44

They Weren't Me

The room was cold as a mid autumn morning.
The memories of us remain here adorning.

The last time we roamed the halls of this house.
That was the last time I'd call you my spouse.

Standing here in this room, no fire in its place.
Seeing only them now as I look upon your face.

It was in this room which I once entered.
To find you there where our love centered.

Only this day you weren't alone.
They weren't me, this wasn't their home.

In that moment I began to see red.
Before I knew it our marriage was dead.

Their name was one I never knew.
Later I would find they were only one of the few.

Who you'd been seeing while I wasn't around.

You'd let me slip out without making a sound.

To the office, or the coffee shop.
If I hadn't found out would this have ever stopped?

45

We Don't Fight Anymore

There was a time when I wasn't sure.
If I could do this with you anymore.

The days grew long, the nights grew colder.
The passing of hours, the strength of a soldier.

Bricks thrown at walls of glass.
Each knocking the other flat on our ass.

Depleting the energy from our souls.
No longer reaching for our goals.

There came a day when we had to choose.
To remain here and fight, or continue to lose.

Knowing then what we had to do.
We gave up the war not knowing what it was for.

In the end, we didn't grow stronger.
Only dragging it out each day a bit longer.

Now we're here some time later.

We don't fight anymore as we've gone our own ways.
To live out the future during brighter days.

46

What A Feeling

What a feeling living in a world with you in it.
Gone are the days of gray tomorrows, and lonesome sorrows.

The horizon of life being stretched like the string of an archers
bow.

You were the arrow which pierced my heart.
Allowing a love to flourish, a relationship to start.

With days no longer bitter, days no longer cold.
Their story was one for generations would be told.

Defying all the odds, yet that's nothing new.
The thing that set apart these two.
Was a monumental shift in societies view.

On love, loss, joy, and suffering.
Rebuilding, rekindling, mustering
the strength to flourish in the face of adversity.

Not caring what they think, feel, or do.
In one another's eyes, there's just you.

The love that one has for the other.
Being all that mattered, and all that was.

What a feeling to be in love.

{ 47 }

When Our Eyes Met

It was over from the moment your eyes met mine.
The feeling I felt, truly divine.

It was something I had yet to feel before.
A feeling so warm, I sank deeply into the floor.

Never wanting to move, nor that feeling to leave.
It was the moment I met you, my soul was relieved.

An instant connection through your eyes.
An awaking of the soul taking me by surprise.

I knew in that moment, I'd just met the rest of my life.
A life with you was all I longed for.

Thank God for allowing that open door.
Which we walked through.

Forever together, never again without you.
When our eyes met was the moment I knew.

48

When You Were Mine

When you were mine I knew your name.
Now that you're gone it isn't the same.

When you were mine I'd gained all there was to gain.
Now that you're gone some days are insane.

When you were mine I'd saw the sun.
Now that you're gone the light is too.

When you were mine I never felt a need to run.
Now that you're gone, I no longer have fun.

When you were mine all felt fine.
Now that you're gone, I've fallen into a void.

When you were mine we'd often go out to dine.
Now that you're gone, I barley consume.

When you were mine I felt complete.
Now that you're gone I can't find my feet.

When you were mine life was divine.

Opposite Ends Of The Arrow

Now that you're gone, I wish you were still mine.

49

Where Were you?

I woke to find no one there.
With the bed still made I searched everywhere.

My hope began to fade, it was happening again.
Where were you? Out with a friend?

Or were you stepping out on me as you had before.
Overwhelmed by the feeling, an explosion within my core.

Collecting my thoughts I wish to say.
Tell me darling, what's their name?

Yet you aren't here so I wait in silence by the phone.
Hoping perhaps I'd receive a call telling me that I was wrong.

Then everything would be okay.
Yet I knew that call wouldn't come, not today anyway...

{ 50 }

Wishing On A Fallen Star

Stars falling from the sky.
Hearts laid bleeding, well ran dry.

How do we get passed this? Where do we go from here?
Is there anywhere safe, where our hearts don't have to fear?

Keeping faith in you is like wishing on a fallen star.
Don't hold your breath, it isn't gonna get you far.

At the first chance advantage is taken.
To put my trust in you, I was mistaken.

As soon as my back was turned.
You went out, and done what you knew better than to do.

How can you sit there as if nothing wrong was done?
Is this some game to you, is this fun?

Sitting back watching, as I live out my days.
All the while knowing you'd gotten away.

With whatever it was that if it were known.

Would have been the final reason for your name etched in stone.

About The Author

"Never mind about me. Focus on the art which I have created,
and remember in life we're never promised a rose garden without thorns."

J.